Original title:
Jungle by the Window

Copyright © 2025 Creative Arts Management OÜ
All rights reserved.

Author: Alexander Thornton
ISBN HARDBACK: 978-1-80581-939-4
ISBN PAPERBACK: 978-1-80581-466-5
ISBN EBOOK: 978-1-80581-939-4

Serenity Through the Frame

Lizards in tuxedos, they strut in a line,
Picking up pizza crumbs, oh, how divine!
A bird in a bow tie sings songs of delight,
While squirrels wear glasses, oh, what a sight!

A monkey with manners sips tea on a chair,
Chasing the butterflies, without a care.
Caterpillars gossip, they twist and they bend,
In this leafy abode, where fun has no end.

Sunlight Dancing on Leaves

The rays perform pirouettes through branches green,
As shadows play tag, a comical scene.
A frog in a top hat leaps high with great flair,
While dragonflies giggle, weaving light through the air.

A sloth holds a party, quite slow and serene,
With snacks made of nectar, oh, isn't it keen?
The ants play the banjo, quite lost in their tune,
As the sun winks at twilight, beneath the big moon.

Journey to the Overgrown

Raccoons on a road trip, packed up in a van,
They stop for a picnic where wildflowers span.
With snacks made of berries, oh, what a feast,
They toast with their drinks, a fruit punch at least.

A snail told a joke, which raced round the bend,
While hedgehogs in capes play superhero friends.
They slide down the hill, oh what a grand trip,
With laughter and antics, they tumble and flip.

Whispers of the Wilderness

The trees share their secrets in rustles and sighs,
While owls in pajamas hoot wise little lies.
A parrot in polka dots makes fashion waves,
As raccoons play bingo, winning with knaves.

The moon is a spotlight on a scene so bizarre,
Where critters are dancing beneath the bright star.
With laughter and cheer, this wild comedy flows,
As friends share their stories, in trunks and in bows.

Embracing Nature's Quiet Solitude

In the chaos, a lizard grins,
Hiding under our fridge's fins.
Watching me cook with great delight,
Who knew my omelet's such a sight?

Birds tweet gossip, sounds so silly,
Squirrels chase like they're in a filly.
The cat jumps up, eyes wide in fright,
Just to find a bug in the light.

Glimpses of Flora and Fauna

A flower peeks through a rusty gate,
It thinks it's bold, but it's just fate.
A bee buzzes with a tiny cheer,
Trying to olé a flower here!

Ferns dance like they're at a ball,
While ants march proud, not small at all.
As I sip tea with quirky grace,
I swear one waved back in my space!

Between Worlds of Nature and Home

My couch is realms where spirits roam,
Yet nature knocks, saying, "I'm home!"
A raccoon peeks, I offer snacks,
We giggle, sharing funny quacks.

The blender whirs, it scares the bees,
They hover by with comical pleas.
Through the glass, they hold a meeting,
Plotting how to keep me fleeting!

The Eyes of the Wilderness

A cat looks out, she's on the prowl,
Her rival? An owl with a scowl.
They throw looks like they're in a play,
Who will win this stare-down today?

A raccoon wobbles, tripping in haste,
He slips on leaves; oh, what a waste!
Nature laughs with joy so bright,
While I chuckle from my cozy sight!

Secrets in the Canopy

Birds in hats play cards at noon,
Swinging leaves hum a silly tune.
Squirrels gossip, tails in the air,
One tries to dance, slips off a chair.

Monkeys wear glasses to read the news,
While frogs leap about in oversized shoes.
The vines twist around like a jolly snake,
Chasing the breeze, causing a quake.

Lush Dreams Beyond Glass

Lizards with ties are throwing a ball,
While snails line up to give it their all.
The peacocks strut in sequined style,
Inviting everyone for a wild, wild mile.

A sloth in pajamas takes quite a nap,
Dreaming of racing, thinking he'll tap.
The stamps on the leaves count their years,
As whispers of laughter drift through the spheres.

The View from the Thicket

Butterflies Cheers! for a tiny parade,
With ants in sunglasses, they aren't afraid.
A raccoon with a snack on a tire swing,
Calls out to everyone, "Come see me bling!"

Camouflaged chameleons try to blend,
While turtles are racing — who'll make the bend?
The clamor of critters echoes and peaks,
As they share their adventures for days and for weeks.

Enchanted Leaves

Dancing twigs in a hilarious tango,
While beetles beat drums like they're in a radio.
A wise old owl tells the best of tales,
As giggles erupt from behind their veils.

Fluttering giggles fill the soft air,
With foxes in bowties showing they care.
The breeze plays tricks like a playful sprite,
Tickling the branches, oh what a sight!

Lush Retreats Beyond Glass

Through smudged panes, I gaze outside,
Where the parrot wears a hat, quite wide.
A squirrel's dance, a wobble with flair,
Who knew acorns had a fashion affair?

Vines creep up with a sneaky twist,
The groundhog peeks – does he know he's missed?
Lizards twirl in a balmy duet,
In this wild show, the fun's not done yet!

The Untamed World Awaits

Bees in tuxedos buzz by my head,
While chattering monkeys plot in their bed.
A snail in a race, oh what a sight,
Whispering secrets of snails in the night.

The wind blows a tune, such a lovely cheer,
A turtle takes off, it's hard to believe here!
Frogs in bow ties sing out of tune,
Dancing to rhythms of mischief and moon.

Green Dreams at Dusk

Fireflies twinkle in a winking spree,
As the grasshopper sings, 'Hey, come dance with me!'
A raccoon with glasses reads by the night,
And sings to the stars with delight so bright.

Leaves rustle secrets, a whispering breeze,
The owl's making jokes, oh don't you want these?
A hedgehog giggles, tucks in for the night,
As laughter and shadows take playful flight.

Nature's Embrace through Panes

From the window, the world seems absurd,
A llama tries yoga, isn't that weird?
An iguana serves tea for a clique of their kind,
As ducks in a row argue who's best to find.

A parade of wildness, all here to see,
With antics and tales that tickle with glee.
Nature's a circus, oh what a show,
Through glass, the laughter continues to flow.

Reflections of Fern and Flower

In a pot, a fern does sprout,
As I trip, my shoe falls out.
A flower plays a game of peek,
With my cat, too shy to speak.

Sunshine dances on the floor,
While my coffee spills once more.
A leaf sways, a breeze strikes bold,
And whispers secrets yet untold.

Soliloquy of the Leaves

Oh, leaf that tickles every nose,
In green attire, you strike a pose.
'Fetch me some water!' cries the vine,
As I wear my shoes that shine.

A rustle, a giggle, here and there,
Frogs in boots, looking quite rare.
With jokes like that, who needs a show?
But watch your step, there's mud below!

Memories of the Wild Side

A lizard's dance amidst the dust,
Claims my heart with purest trust.
Chasing shadows in a whirl,
Socks mismatched like a twirling girl.

A chitter-chat from the leafy mess,
Makes my brain feel quite a stress.
But who can frown in this bright glade?
When giggles echo, worries fade!

Songs of the Untouched

With a wink, the petals sway,
As butterflies join in the play.
One landed on my nose, oh dear!
In this calm, nothing to fear.

Dancing whispers fill the air,
A squirrel laughs without a care.
With every pitter-patter sound,
My rhythm in this world is found.

The Lure of the Great Outdoors

In the backyard, nature calls,
With twigs and sticks as mighty walls.
Squirrels plot with acorn plans,
While ants march on in little bands.

A leaf canopy of dusty hue,
Offers shade for a game or two.
The dog wears a hat, quite absurd,
While the cat pretends she's not perturbed.

O grasshoppers leap, and crickets sing,
What joy does this weirdness bring!
I shout at clouds, they seem to laugh,
As butterflies tease with a cheeky gaff.

Beneath the trees, I twirl and spin,
Tripping on roots—let the fun begin!
Nature's laughter echoes afar,
In this eccentric backyard bazaar.

Reflections on a Canopy of Leaves

Sunlight filters through leafy crowns,
As I dodge the raindrops like clowns.
Pine cones drop with a thud and roll,
Nature's mischief takes its toll.

A squirrel sneaks peeks at my snack,
Thinking twice, then starts the attack.
With a wobble and a little pirouette,
He steals my chips and runs off, you bet!

Birds gossip loudly, what a show!
While I argue with a bush about dough.
Caught in the antics, I grin wide,
In this wild place, jokes seem to collide.

Chasing shadows that dance at my feet,
Nature's puzzled, but can't be beat.
Leaves whisper secrets like silly bards,
In this leafy realm, no one keeps guards.

Whispers of the Green

The garden's a stage, a comic play,
With worms doing tango, hip hip hooray!
A dandelion fluffs its golden fluff,
While a gopher picks fights, oh, that's tough!

In the midst of flowers, smells so sweet,
Comes a raccoon who thinks it's a treat.
I attempt a chat; he just blinks slow,
Then scampers off as if saying, 'No!'

A bees' buzzing chorus is all around,
And I get lost in this playful sound.
A snail races by on a slippery quest,
But little does he know he's quite the jest.

The sun waves hello, the clouds roll away,
Nature's antics light up the day.
With every rustle and giggle so bright,
Laughter erupts in this green delight!

Veils of the Verdant

Underneath the leafy shade,
The squirrels host a grand parade.
With nuts as hats and tails held high,
They lead a jig as birds fly by.

The critters chat; it sounds like rhymes,
Trading puns, oh what fun times!
A hedgehog joins with little spins,
As laughter breaks upon the winds.

Bushes gossip, giggles abound,
While daisies nod in harmony sound.
A bear steals a seat, but oh so shy,
With a grin that could light up the sky.

In the muddle of mischief, I place my bets,
On who wins the race—although no regrets.
Nature's a joker wearing her crown,
In this canopy life, we all clown around.

A Tantalizing Glimpse

Monkeys peek through the curtain,
With eyes full of curiosity,
Swinging around like little acrobats,
Making our day a comedy.

A parrot mimics my loud sneeze,
While a gecko photobombs the scene,
Every rustle brings a giggle,
Nature's antics are so keen.

A shy sloth hangs in a tree,
Slow-motion antics, pure delight,
It waves hello with a lazy arm,
Just a trickster in the light.

In this vibrant, leafy show,
Life dances like a silly reel,
With creatures bringing joy and laughs,
Who said nature can't be ideal?

Shadows and Sunshine in Harmony

Laughter echoes through the leaves,
As the sun slips in to play,
The shadows twirl, a guessing game,
Hiding where the bright lights sway.

A bug gets lost in endless chatter,
Complaining loudly to a bee,
"Where's the nectar? This is madness!"
And everybody hears with glee.

A turtle takes his morning stroll,
With all the speed of a quaint dream,
Crowd of critters cheering loud,
For this slowpoke on his beam.

In this realm of quirky sights,
Every moment's like a jest,
Nature's joy is loud and bright,
In this madness, we are blessed.

When Leaves Paint the Windows

Colors splash across the glass,
Each leaf seems to play a part,
A squirrel's stunt brings laughs galore,
As nature crafts its funny art.

Blowing breezes tease the branches,
As a raccoon tiptoes by,
Looking for snacks in the flowerbeds,
With a sneaky, sideways spy.

The sunlight tickles every stem,
While shadows dance like playful kids,
Together they form a merry game,
Where nobody knows what each did.

As I sit and sip my brew,
With laughter ringing, time stands still,
This canvas of green, bright and true,
Fills the heart with a happy thrill.

Lullabies of the Green World

A croaking frog starts off the tune,
With crickets adding their own beat,
They form a band beneath the stars,
 Creating music, oh so sweet.

A firefly joins for some bright flair,
 Blinking like a tiny light show,
While a raccoon rolls down the hill,
With giggles chasing both so slow.

The dawn arrives with roosters crowing,
As sunbeams peek through tangled vines,
 Nature's laugh is everywhere,
 In a world where joy entwines.

A symphony, both loud and cheery,
As critters croon their carefree song,
 In this wild and leafy cradle,
Life's melody feels like play all day long.

An Unseen Garden's Tale

Amidst the green, a lizard grins,
While ants debate on where to begin.
A parrot squawks a joke so loud,
The flowers giggle, feeling proud.

A frog in boots, so fancy and spry,
Tries to hop high, but hits a pie.
The bees do a dance, all in a flare,
While snails are stuck, going nowhere.

A butterfly flutters, wearing a hat,
As crickets chirp, 'What of that?'
The sun smiles down, a mischievous glow,
Painting the scene with a vibrant show.

In this lively place of humor and fun,
Every critter plays, under the sun.
So come along, don't miss the thrill,
For nature's laughter, you can't distill.

Nature's Pendant at Dawn

A squirrel juggles nuts with great flair,
While foxes gossip about who's got hair.
The flowers yawn, stretching wide,
Dreaming of dew drops that tickle and slide.

A snail on a skateboard zooms down the lane,
While a raccoon chuckles, sipping rain.
"Who needs a car when you can glide?"
The trees sway gently, their leaves filled with pride.

The morning sun winks, pulls up a chair,
As mushrooms pop out, pretending to dare.
The whole forest sings, a raucous delight,
As critters all dance till the fall of night.

Laughter rolls through the woods, a soft sound,
In nature's pendant, joy can be found.
Join the fun, let your worries go,
For in this haven, all spirits glow.

The Living Canvas of the World

A pelican paints with a splash of glee,
While monkeys swing, oh so carefree.
The daisies prance in a colorful row,
As rainbows play a game of peek-a-boo show.

The earthworms draw maps with squiggly lines,
While beetles craft tales on leafy pines.
A hedge of ivy whispers bright tales,
Of chasing the wind and riding the gales.

Cacti wear hats, like a cactus parade,
As sunflowers giggle in their bright shade.
The wind joins in, a whimsical cheer,
As creatures unite, bringing laughter near.

In this wild art, every moment's a thrill,
With colors and songs, the heart to fill.
Let's dance with the leaves, twirl with the air,
For life's a canvas, so splash everywhere.

Sanctuary in the Verdant Mist

In a room with plants that swirl,
They're plotting, scheming, give a twirl.
A fern gives side-eye, so profound,
While a pothos lounges all around.

The cactus, prickly, grins so wide,
Beneath it, the dust bunnies can hide.
A bromeliad sends a cheeky wink,
As if to say, 'You really stink!'

A squirrel outside throws acorns in,
While the ivy shakes with a laugh, a grin.
The sunlight spills with a sizzling cheer,
In this place, there's nothing to fear.

So here's to this green, lively scene,
Where dreams of mischief create the sheen.
Plants whisper secrets, oh what a thrill,
In our verdant mist, we always will!

The Call of the Overgrown

Oh, the plush ferns wave and frolic,
While I attempt to look quite stoic.
A gecko pops out, doing a dance,
And I can't help but join in the chance!

Vines dangle low, like they're trying to tease,
Entwining my feet, as if to say 'Please!'
The rubber plant plays the king of the tome,
While I sit here, far from my home.

Wild undergrowth calls with a giggle and cheer,
And a mischievous parakeet caws loud and clear.
Everywhere there's a tangle of green,
In this chaos, my heart feels so keen.

Oh, laughter erupts from leaves rustling near,
As I trip over roots, nothing to fear.
This call of the wild, oh so divine,
In my leafy realm, everything's fine!

Fragments of a Hidden Realm

In the corners, shadows dance and sway,
While the potting soil starts to play.
Tiny creatures skitter, having a ball,
In our fragmented world, they invite us all.

Raccoons at the window trade jokes so sly,
While a sunflower giggles and waves goodbye.
Mushrooms giggle, sprouting under the light,
In this odd realm, things feel just right.

The petals conspire to craft a grand scheme,
As the rubber tree rolls with a chuckling dream.
Its leaves whisper tales of mischief and mirth,
In this hidden realm, we find our worth.

Here, laughter blooms like a wildflower spree,
With each burst of joy, we claim our decree.
Fragments unite in a crazy parade,
In this secret space, never afraid!

The Dance of Sunbeams and Ferns

Sunbeams tumble through the lively greens,
Casting shadows like playful scenes.
The ferns sway gently, a graceful ballet,
While I sip tea, thinking, 'What a day!'

A quirky beetle dons a tiny bow,
As he struts his stuff, putting on a show.
Glittering dust swirls through the air,
In this radiant dance, nothing's quite fair.

Laughter bubbles from the leafy expanse,
As I twirl with the sun in a fanciful dance.
The jade plant hums a merry tune,
With petals swirling like a whimsical moon.

So let's celebrate this sunny delight,
Where whimsy runs rampant, our hearts feel light.
In this joyous display, we all take turns,
In the dance of the sunbeams and ferns!

Captured Wildness

In a garden, vines do wriggle,
My cat thinks he can out-swiggle.
Lizards play tag on the fence,
While I laugh at their common sense.

Butterflies dance in the breeze,
My snacks getting stolen by bees.
Who knew that a flower could sway,
And hurl all my lunch away?

Squirrels plot from their lofty trees,
Daring each other to steal my peas.
With acorns as helmets, they dive,
In this mad world, I feel alive!

A mystery grows beneath the leaves,
While froggies croak their witty thieves.
Nature's roles are simply too funny,
As I chase my cat, and he finds honey!

A Canvas of Nature's Palette

Colors explode where eyes can see,
Daisies gossip with a bumblebee.
The trees all wear their greenest ties,
While bright red ants plot their pie in the sky.

Painting the world with a splash of zest,
Even the cacti get dressed to impress.
While flowers pose with a playful flair,
I can't help but stop and stare!

A colorful parrot sings a tune,
While I dance with shadows of the moon.
Every petal tells a joke to be told,
As nature winks in shades of gold.

Little critters scurry and race,
With painted wings—oh, what a chase!
In this riot of hues, I feel elated,
In a world where art is celebrated!

The Breath of Untamed Life

Whiskers twitch while I sip tea,
As rabbits bounce, they flirt with glee.
With every sip, a leaf might fly,
While squirrels flaunt their newest tie.

A curious raccoon snatches my fries,
Its masked face shows such sly surprise.
The wind carries chuckles from a tree,
As branches jiggle, feeling free.

A snake in shades of disco moves,
In this wild dance, nothing removes.
I bust a move, hoping to impress,
With limbs that clearly need some rest.

Through laughter and squeaks, I hear the tone,
Of creatures laughing at my awkward bone.
In this breath of chaos, life runs rife,
Where every wiggle cuts like a knife!

Nature's Symphony Beyond the Frame

Amidst the leaves, a chorus peaks,
Birds chirp Sonatas; oh, what freaks!
While crickets tap out a jazzy beat,
Nature's band is so hard to seat!

The sun drops in for a shining guest,
Lighting up each critter's quest.
A raccoon conducts with stylish flair,
Twirling its baton, without a care!

The frogs join in with a ribbit rhyme,
While ants commingle, keeping time.
Flower petals clap in admiration,
Each hue adding its own narration.

With laughter as the rhythm flows,
And giggles popping like bows!
This silly show, a grand charade,
In this wild tune, my worries fade!

Harmony in the Overgrowth

In a tangle of leaves, the parrot squawks loud,
A squirrel in pajamas, he's quite the proud.
Swinging on vines, with a wacky spree,
He dances like nobody, just wait and see!

The monkey with goggles climbs up all the way,
A self-proclaimed pilot, he rules the day.
He slips on a fruit, oh what a big splash,
Now he's stuck in a puddle, oh what a crash!

Crickets hold concerts with a tap-tap beat,
While frogs in tuxedos take over the street.
Together they frolic in splendid delight,
Under the glow of the mushroom's soft light.

Laughter erupts from the hedges nearby,
As a hedgehog does cartwheels, oh me, oh my!
Nature's own circus, where chaos does reign,
In the land of the funny, there's never a bane.

Blossoms of a Forgotten Realm

In the garden of giggles where daisies chatter,
A rabbit named Benny is climbing a ladder.
He hops to the top to survey his domain,
And slips on a petal, oh what a plain!

The bees wear bowties, buzzing with flair,
While butterflies twirl without a single care.
They sip on sweet nectar, a fancy buffet,
With cupcakes and cookies on a sunny day.

A tortoise in spectacles reads a fine book,
While frogs sip on tea with a delicate look.
Giggling and gossiping about the day's quests,
The winks and the nods become their own tests.

Laughter erupts from a pumpkin parade,
As a corn cob played fiddle, the jokes were well-made.
In this mix of mirth, where silliness thrives,
Every creature dances, oh how it arrives!

Emerald Hues Dancing in Time

In a tapestry woven with bright shades of green,
The sloths take a dance, oh what a scene!
Swinging from branches, they sway so slow,
While chattering monkeys put on quite a show.

Snakes wear their stripes like a fashionable trend,
Slithering sideways to the beats that they send.
With a shimmy and shake, they're life's little jest,
In this wriggly rhythm, we're all supremely blessed.

A parade of the curious creeps through the glades,
As fireflies twinkle with sparkles that fade.
Giggling with each step, the shadows do roam,
In this bright emerald hue, we all feel at home.

With every bright chuckle, a leaf starts to sway,
Together with laughter, they dance the night away.
In this carnival bright, where joy takes its prime,
A riddle of humor, forever in rhyme!

Ties of Earth and Sky

In the chatter of crickets beneath the tall trees,
A raccoon named Benny bakes biscuits with ease.
He sprinkles the dough with a pinch of delight,
As owls join the fun under silvery light.

A kangaroo hops through a puddle contrived,
With splashes of laughter, the whole crew survives.
They gather around for a feast on the grass,
As fireflies twinkle, the moments will last.

A turtle on roller skates zooms by with a grin,
While squirrels on unicycles join in the din.
Bouncing and skidding, oh what a display,
In the ties of their laughter, we all want to play!

In a sky painted pink as the sun bids goodbye,
The creatures of mirth share a wink and a sigh.
For in this fine realm where the wilds intertwine,
Life's greatest pleasure is humor divine!

Echoes of the Untamed

Chirping critters dance around,
As I munch on toast, quite profound.
A squirrel peers through, full of cheer,
Wondering why I'm stuck right here.

Lively vines weave tales untold,
Where laughter blooms, and fun unfolds.
A parrot squawks, my jokes are lame,
Yet still, it joins my quirky game.

Wiggly worms in search of fun,
Twist and turn, then come undone.
While frogs croak tunes in a band,
I try to clap with buttered hands.

Oh, morning glories blush and tease,
As ants march on, with expert ease.
They never stop, they never tire,
While I'm here, just snacking higher.

The Realm of Ferns and Vines

In a tangled maze, I trip and fall,
A spider laughs, 'Oh, what a sprawl!'
The ferns are dancing, they can't be tamed,
As I attempt to strut unashamed.

A raccoon peeks, with a cheeky grin,
Stealing my lunch, where do I begin?
Vines swing low, making their calls,
I grab my hat, prevent it from falls.

Grasshoppers hop like little clowns,
Each jump a joke, as they bounce around.
With every leap, they cheer and shout,
While I just grin, a welcome tout.

Sunlight filters, humor's the game,
With leafy friends who know my name.
In this wild realm, I'm never alone,
A party grows, like bright flowers, grown.

Fragments of the Wild World

Butterflies flutter, colors collide,
Chasing their dreams, with nothing to hide.
Meanwhile, I bee-bop, twirl and sway,
As frogs give me tips, 'Just dance this way!'

The breeze whispers jokes, oh so absurd,
Trees snicker low, it's quite the herd.
With branches bending, they join the jest,
While I'm there, putting laughter to test.

Glimmers of mischief, everywhere found,
Creatures convene in a merry-go-round.
The world spins round, like a dizzying game,
In every nook, it's all the same.

From toads to tigers, quips start to grow,
In this vivid ballet, there's no sign of slow.
United in laughter, quite foolish and free,
A wild world blooming, just fragrant glee.

Solitude Among the Foliage

In shadows deep, I sip my drink,
While chipmunks offer snacks, I think.
A sloth drapes down, in cozy pose,
With sleepy smiles and wiggly toes.

A breeze begins to whisper 'round,
Telling secrets that do astound.
The leaves giggle, 'What an odd sight!'
As I hum along, feeling quite light.

With whispers shared, my thoughts take flight,
While creatures plot mischief, into the night.
A snake slides by with poise and charm,
Yet in my heart, there's no cause for alarm.

The secret life of vines and trees,
Brings laughter like a gentle breeze.
In solitude found, there's joy to be made,
With nature's fun, I'm never afraid.

Shadows on the Sill

A cat once danced on my sill,
Chasing shadows, oh what a thrill!
It leaped and pounced, struck a pose,
Then fell off, right on its nose!

The plants would giggle, rustle leaves,
While birds peeked in with little thieves.
The sun would wink, and I would laugh,
What a circus, my own photograph!

Sometimes a bug would join the fun,
Flapping around, thinking it's won.
But with one swipe, the cat was quick,
Brought the show down with rhythmic flick!

So here I sit, in my leafy room,
With silent giggles, the plants in bloom.
Life's a merry game, on every sill,
With shadows laughing, and time to kill!

Nature's Breath in Silence

Outside my house, the squirrels play,
Making mischief through the day.
They chase each other, zig and zag,
In the corner, an old rag!

The birds hold meetings, up so high,
Plotting ways to sneak and fly.
Each beak tells tales of snacks nearby,
As I sip tea and let out a sigh.

A sleepy raccoon drifts by at noon,
With a wink that suggests it's up to tune.
It tiptoes past, a master thief,
I chuckle softly, what a belief!

In silence, the wild seems to laugh,
Nature's antics, a joyful craft.
Birdsong echoes, as life unfolds,
In this quiet show, just as it holds!

Hues of the Hidden Wild

In my garden, colors dance bright,
Bees steal nectar, what a sight!
With a twist and a twirl, they spin,
Like they're in some buzzing din!

The flowers gossip, petals ablaze,
Sharing secrets in flowery ways.
Sunflowers nod in merry jest,
While daisies don their polka-dots best!

A frog in green, jumps with flair,
Landing softly without a care.
It croaks a tune, quite out of sync,
Alongside a chipmunk, who's on the brink!

In hues of joy, the wild speaks free,
Nature's palette, a sight to see.
Life's a canvas, painted with smiles,
Mirth and madness stretching for miles!

A Glimpse of Wilderness

Behind the glass, a world ablaze,
With buzzing critters in a daze.
A scuffle, a tumble, oh what a show!
Nature's antics, on the go!

The dogs bark wildly, chasing scents,
In their heads, grand events commence.
A lizard darts, in camouflage,
A daring escape, a small mirage!

Chickens cluck in their feathery suits,
Debating the world's tastiest fruits.
I sip my coffee, giggling so loud,
At the small wild hearts, nature's crowd!

With laughter and wonder, I look outside,
Where wildness and humor easily glide.
A glimpse of joy, a slice of cheer,
Through my window, the wild draws near!

Beyond the Urban Veil

In the concrete maze, a monkey pranks,
Swinging right over the traffic ranks.
He steals a burger, oh what a sight,
As pigeons squawk in a feathery fright.

A lizard slides down the subway stairs,
Wearing sunglasses, without any cares.
It stops for a moment, strikes a pose,
In the city chaos, its fashion just glows.

A rhino in slippers strolls through the park,
Making friendships with dogs as it barks.
The squirrels just giggle, oh what a show,
As taxis honk loudly, a bustling flow.

Cacti with hats wave hello to the crowd,
Trees dance their tango, they're feeling quite proud.
In this urban jungle, fun knows no end,
Where city meets nature, and laughter transcends.

Soft Sounds of the Leafy Realm

In a garden of whispers, the frogs tune their socks,
While beetles in bow ties do the moonwalk on rocks.
A snail takes a selfie, slow-motion swag,
As ants bring confetti, what a vibrant brag!

The flowers throw shade on the buzzing bees,
As they gossip and giggle with floating hot breeze.
A parrot in colors calls its friends near,
But all that they hear is a boisterous cheer.

Butterflies dance in a floral parade,
While worms do the worm in the sunlight cascade.
The daisies poke fun at the gophers below,
Who dig up the soil with a comedic show.

At twilight they gather, a leafy conspire,
With shadows in laughter, they light up the fire.
In this soft symphony, each note's a delight,
As nature creates music in magical night.

The Comfort of Green Shadows

In the niche of the garden, a raccoon can't hide,
With snacks in its paws and a mischievous pride.
At dusk it dances, all wiggly and round,
The neighbors all laugh, it's the best show in town!

A tree with a beard tosses leaves like confetti,
While the wind joins the chorus, its rhythm so jetty.
A hedgehog detective seeks clues on the run,
But all that he finds is a berry for fun.

A cat in a hammock, so cool and so sly,
Pretends to be snoozing, with one open eye.
While chirpy young crickets provide the right beat,
As the night turns to magic, a humorous feat.

The moon in its splendor smiles down at the play,
As shadows stretch out in a light-hearted way.
In this cuddly cocoon, giggles echo so free,
Where comfort is found in lighthearted glee.

Echoes of Life Beyond Barriers

In an alleyway garden, the gnomes hold a feast,
While cats share their tales of adventures, at least.
A plant with a party hat sways to the bay,
As mischievous winds sweep the boredom away.

The goldfish swim circles with stories to tell,
About escapades bubbling, oh they know it so well!
A frog in a tuxedo croons to the stars,
While fireflies twinkle like shimmering bars.

Squirrels perform acrobatics with flair,
As branches applaud with a rustling cheer.
An octopus dreams of a life in the sea,
But here in this realm, it's just fancy and free.

The laughter of daisies fills up the night air,
As shadows play games, without any care.
In this realm of giggles that nobody charts,
The echoes of life paint smiles in their hearts.

Beyond the Barrier of Glass

The chattering monkeys want to play,
They swing and leap without a say.
I sip my tea, they tease me so,
Their goofy faces steal the show.

A parrot squawks with such delight,
It mocks my hair, oh what a sight!
I laugh and point, they turn away,
Then mimic me all through the day.

The foghorn toads croak from afar,
While I just sip my lemonade jar.
With every ribbit, my giggles rise,
They make me laugh, what a surprise!

Through glass, we meet, yet never touch,
The wild ones here, they laugh so much.
Who knew that nature would inspire,
Such silly times, a funny choir!

Treetops and Twilight

The squirrels dance in their frantic spree,
As if there's an acorn jubilee!
They spin and twirl, all without a clue,
While I just sip cocoa, feeling blue.

A little fox sneaks up to peek,
With bushy tail, he's such a sneak.
He trips on roots, oh what a scene,
I laugh so hard, I spill my green!

At dusk, the birds put on a show,
With silly songs that make me glow.
They chirp and flap, in wild delight,
Creating tunes that make my night.

Soon dreams will bloom, as stars ignite,
The creatures whisper, "Insects take flight!"
Yet here I sit, content and warm,
With nature's antics, my heart's at charm.

Fluttering Wings in the Quiet

The butterflies flutter with flair so bold,
With colors grand, they dance in gold.
They tease the flowers with delicate grace,
While I just giggle, what a funny race!

A bumblebee hums a silly tune,
It's tripping over blooms like a swoon.
I wave and cheer, "You've got no rhyme!"
But he bumbles back, "I'm busy, in prime!"

The lizards lounge on a sunlit rock,
While playing tag, they seem to mock.
I watch them smile from ear to ear,
What a game, oh, let's give a cheer!

In this lovely space, where laughter sings,
Nature's jokes are the best of things.
So here's to fun, both wild and free,
In moments spent by me and thee!

Nature's Lullaby at Dusk

As shadows stretch, the frogs commence,
A concert loud, oh what suspense!
They ribbit rhythm with quirky flair,
As I just chuckle, fireflies flare.

The owls hoot, in a way so sage,
But their jokes just seem to set the stage.
They flap and blink, in humorous tune,
While I chuckle softly beneath the moon.

The raccoons gather for a feast,
With popcorn here, it's just a beast!
They nibble and giggle, such a sight,
Their party makes my evening bright.

With nature's laughter filling the air,
Each sound and sight's beyond compare.
A lullaby of joy, oh what a dream,
In this wild world, where giggles gleam!

Echoes of the Rainforest

Frogs with hats, they sing so loud,
Monkeys dance, oh look at that crowd!
Parrots squawk in colorful glee,
Twirling like dancers, wild and free.

Giant lilies with rosy cheeks,
Wobble and giggle, they love to tease.
The air is thick with laughter's sound,
Swinging from limbs, joy knows no bounds.

The Allure of Nature's Embrace

Lizards strutting in striped bow ties,
Caterpillars wearing sweet surprise.
Squirrels on stilts, they're quite the sight,
Wobbling left, then taking flight.

A breeze brings whispers of silly tales,
While crickets play their tiny scales.
With apples cascading from trees above,
Each one a piece of laughter and love.

Breaths of Fresh Vibrance

Rats in capes, oh what a show,
Zipping by like they know they glow.
A snake in sneakers, slithers with flair,
Chasing a snail, oh please beware!

Sunset paints the critters so bold,
With jokes exchanged, the stories told.
Even the ants throw a little dance,
Kick up their feet, take a chance!

The Hidden Life Beyond Sight

Termites in tuxedos tap their feet,
While bees do a jig to the funky beat.
Each branch a stage, each leaf a seat,
Mother Nature's comedy can't be beat.

Bugs with shades, sipping on dew,
Critters play games, just for a view.
In this hub of mirth, secrets twine,
Each corner a laugh, each moment divine.

Mysteries Beneath the Sunlight

A squirrel in a fedora, quite the sight,
Dances with a lizard, both take flight.
Sunbeams play tag on bright green leaves,
While cheeky monkeys weave silly eaves.

A breeze whispers secrets, oh so clear,
As insects hold conferences, laugh and jeer.
Toads wear bowties, looking very spry,
As butterflies giggle, oh me, oh my!

Rabbits in glasses read novels, so spry,
While cats in capes soar through the sky.
Each creature adds color to this wild stage,
A colorful cast on nature's bright page.

Together they frolic, a whimsical blend,
In a vivid world, where laughter won't end.
With sunlight ticking the time in this play,
In a playful parade where the wild things stay.

Enigma of the Wilderness

A raccoon with a map, quite confused,
Searches for treasure, a bit bemused.
While fireflies hold lanterns, they define,
A path through melodrama, a quirky line.

The parrot's gossip spills like hot tea,
On squirrels in tuxedos, sipping green brie.
Laughter erupts, as shadows just jig,
Stealing the limelight, they dance a big jig.

Tents made of leaves, fashioned with care,
Create cozy rooms for the critters to share.
In the twilight glow, they swap funny tales,
Of daring escapades, of mischief and fails.

So come, raise a toast to the oddest crew,
In a world of wander where odd things ensue.
Here, enigmas wrap joy in a playful tryst,
In the wilderness, where none could resist.

Light Filtering Through Green

Beams filter in like a golden surprise,
As striped snakes play peek-a-boo, oh, they're wise!
Frogs croak in rhythm; a band out of tune,
As shadows leap dance like children in June.

Under the ferns, a gnome flips a flap,
With a grin on his face, in a snug little gap.
The edge of a leaf creates dramatic flair,
Hosting a party for a dragonfly pair.

Sunlight chuckles while bunnies hop round,
Wrestling with daisies, lost in the sound.
Each ray brings laughter, a playful delight,
Making green giggle from morning till night!

So lean in closely, soak up the fun,
In this leafy place where whimsy's begun.
With light shining bright, banishing gloom,
Let's dance with the shadows and make the room bloom.

The Grace of Unseen Flora

An orchid in a bonnet, sporting fine flair,
Twirling with daisies, showing they care.
Under their petals, a party does dwell,
With whispers of roses casting a spell.

A cactus in sneakers joins the parade,
While tulips tell jokes that easily fade.
Breezes tickle both roots and the tops,
As laughter erupts in their colorful shops.

Unseen, yet they revel, with petals so grand,
In a garden of giggles, hand in hand.
Their jokes are a riot, though not always clear,
Yet blooms and bright colors draw us all near.

So step into this world, just lift up your gaze,
Where flora is funny, and silliness stays.
United in laughter, their spirits will soar,
In this whimsical land, forever and more.

A Mosaic of Foliage

A creature on a branch sings songs,
With socks on its ears and a wig that belongs.
It jigs with the breeze, all furry and spry,
Swinging and flinging, oh my, oh my!

The leaves chuckle softly, in hues of bright green,
While squirrels tell secrets of nut-filled cuisine.
A sloth on the swing grins wide with delight,
It's party time now, till the fall of the night!

The vines twist in laughter, they sway to the beat,
Two turtles in shades take a break from their feet.
They toast with a berry, their friendship so grand,
In this patch of the wild, life's never too planned!

A toucan with style wears a hat made of twigs,
He dances with frogs who leap like they're pigs.
The plot thickens here, with joy to expound,
In this colorful chaos, fun just abounds!

Fragrant Whispers from Outside

The scent of warm chocolate drifts through the air,
As critters form lines, each with their own flair.
A parade of oddities, singing a tune,
While a raccoon plays bongo underneath the moon!

The flowers are gossiping, oh what a treat,
About a grasshopper's dance and a squirrel's quick feet.
A bee with a crown buzzes tales of delight,
While ants in tuxedos prepare for the night!

Mossy shoes are worn by a jumpy young frog,
As he splashes through puddles, all muddy and bogged.
A snail on a skateboard zooms past with a shout,
This fragrant escape makes all worries pout!

A vibrant cacophony, bright colors galore,
Laughter erupts from each leafy front door.
In this fragrant domain, where giggles are found,
Life's a sweet melody, silliness abound!

The Call of the Untamed

From the treetop teeter-totter, a parrot lets fly,
With a joke for the toucan who can't help but sigh.
The monkeys all chuckle, in their fuzzy old homes,
As lizards wear hats made of brown elder cones.

An owl cracked a pun that fell flat on the ground,
It hooted and wobbled, a mischief profound.
With laughter contagious, as wild as a gale,
In the shadows, the beetles enact a small tale!

Under leaves that are giggling, life stirs with a cheer,
A hedgehog in shades waves to the passerby deer.
Squirrels toss acorns like balls in a game,
While a lizard shows moves that puts dancers to shame!

The moonlight glimmers, it's a mischievous night,
Creatures unite for a whimsical fight.
With rumbles and tumbles, they'll flip and they'll fall,
In this call of the wild, joy bubbles for all!

Secrets of the Leafy Escape

Rustling leaves hold secrets, a giggle or two,
As the skunks plan a surprise, for the comfiest crew.
A rabbit in polka dots hops to the show,
In tap shoes and charm, with a radiant glow!

A long line of geckos wear shades made of glass,
As they slide down the branches—oh, how they pass!
Frogs hold a rally on lily pads tight,
Discussing the merits of bugs, day or night.

A wise old chameleon speaks low of the trees,
While squirrels share gossip on world-famous cheese.
The owls hold their breath, while raccoons just grin,
In this leafy escape, it's where fun begins!

The fruits hang so sweet, they chuckle and tease,
While the vines sway along with the soft summer breeze.
In this whimsical wonder, so silly yet bright,
The secrets unfold, bringing pure delight!

Whispers of the Green Veil

In the corner, vines make a scene,
Lizards sport hats, oh so obscene.
Frogs in tuxedos, ready to prance,
Chasing the bugs in a silly dance.

A parrot shouts, 'It's a party time!'
While squirrels compete in a rhythm rhyme.
Bamboo shoots tap like they own the floor,
Laughter resounds, who could ask for more?

The sun peeks in, with a sly little grin,
Echoing giggles from where we begin.
A cat with a monocle, sipping his tea,
Claims he's the king, oh, is that true, we see?

The breeze carries whispers from leaves so bright,
As the ants march in, with their tiny might.
Join in the fun, there's room for all,
In this wild gala, come one, come all!

Shadows in the Canopy

A turtle in shades, lounging with flair,
While cheeky raccoons throw popcorn in air.
The shadows dance, with a wink and a spin,
As monkeys drop in for a mischievous win.

Mice wear capes, acting like stars,
Sipping on nectar from odd-looking jars.
The groundhog juggles, he's quite the hit,
While a spider crochets, with perfect wit.

Among the brambles, a cacophony hums,
The bushy-tailed band strikes hilarious drums.
With twinkling eyes, the gophers all cheer,
As the sun overhead starts to disappear.

Through candle-lit leaves, a giggle resounds,
Inviting us in to the laughter it pounds.
So come take a peek, there's magic in sight,
In the dappled and shadowed, it's always a delight!

Secrets of the Sun-Dappled Room

A sloth on the shelf plays tunes on a flute,
While insects join in, looking quite cute.
Sunbeams like ribbons twirl in the air,
As butterflies gossip, without any care.

Beneath all the colors, a secret is kept,
A dance with no rules, around which they leapt.
The ants look puzzled, scratching their heads,
As a crab wears a crown, sitting on threads.

Chirping and squeaking, a band in full swing,
Wombats chime in, while frogs softly sing.
At twilight's soft blush, the laughter grows loud,
As shadows and whispers form a merry crowd.

In this luminous place, remember to grin,
For the fun ever after is where we begin.
A playful embrace, in a world so bright,
Keep the joy close, till the end of the night!

Echoes of the Wild Outside

With feet in the grass, we hear them all cheer,
The clamor and chaos draws everybody near.
A dog in a bowtie spins like a top,
While cats breakdance, and laughter won't stop.

A hedgehog plays poker, with acorns as chips,
While the owl deals cards with wise little quips.
The rabbits jump high, claiming first prize,
In a silly leap contest, oh, what a surprise!

The wind carries tales of our playful brigade,
As creatures unite for a grand escapade.
With shadows and laughter all dancing around,
A joyful ruckus, in magic we're bound.

So lean out the window, join in on the fun,
For the tales of this wild, we can never outrun.
With giggles and grins, the echoes persist,
In the heart of the wild, we can't help but exist!

Forest Spirits on the Edge

In the forest, where the squirrels play,
Ghosts of laughter dance in the day.
A raccoon in boots steals a snack,
While a gnome wonders, "What's wrong with my hat?"

The trees have hats, all striped and bright,
Waving their branches, a comical sight.
A frog wearing glasses croaks out a tune,
As the bumblebees buzz, making a cartoon.

Up in the branches, squirrels debate,
Who ate the last nut? They can't cooperate.
A wise old owl gives a hoot from above,
"Oh, for heaven's sake, just share the love!"

The path is lined with giggles and smiles,
Where every critter walks in funny styles.
In this wild place, nothing is bland,
As the spirits laugh, and life's all planned.

Dreaming in Shades of Green

In a realm where the kaleidoscope twirls,
A turtle dreams of fancy pearls.
A disco dance with moonlight beams,
As fireflies join in glittering schemes.

Lush leaves whisper secrets so absurd,
A parrot squawks out and gets unheard.
"Oh look, a snail! Did he wear a tie?"
"Of course not, silly! He'll just slip by!"

The bushes chuckle, tickled by fun,
As shadows play hopscotch, one by one.
With laughter echoing softly around,
In shades of green, joy can be found.

Pancakes fly from branches above,
While owls declare, "We're all made of love!"
The night wraps in giggles and glee,
In this green dreamland, wild and free.

Whispers in the Thicket

In the thicket where the whispers twine,
A hedgehog juggles acorns, oh so fine!
A heron slips, looking quite bemused,
As a chipmunk laughs, ever so amused.

Leaves gossip softly beneath the moon,
Frogs sing duets, a charming tune.
A firefly flashes, calling for friends,
As raccoons dance, making amends.

"Who took the snacks?!" squeaks a bold hare,
"Let's split the pranks if you dare!"
A rustle reveals a cheeky young fox,
Wearing a hat made of cardboard and socks.

The thicket hums with life and jest,
Where animals gather to share their quest.
With humor unfolding, nature's the stage,
It's a whimsical world at every age.

The Aroma of Earthy Breaths

Sniff the air, a curious smell,
Is it cookies or magic? Who can tell?
Mushrooms giggle, talkative and spry,
While a rabbit hops by, asking, "Why?"

The dirt has secrets, earthy and sweet,
A hedgehog walks on tiny, furry feet.
A vine grows tangled, laughing at fate,
"Who wears such shoes? Mine are first-rate!"

Beneath the ferns, a party unfolds,
With lizards donning capes, so bold.
"Let's have a feast!" calls a chipper young bee,
As leaves drop confetti, just wait and see!

The aroma of life swirls all around,
Funny little critters make joyous sounds.
In this merry garden, every breath's bright,
In earthy laughter, the heart takes flight.

A Glimpse of Untamed Realms

In a corner, vines creep close,
A monkey steals my comfy pose.
Lizards dance on sunlit beams,
While I plot my wildest dreams.

A parrot peeks in with a glare,
Screaming secrets, do I dare?
Squirrels laugh at my surprise,
As I sip my juice and sigh.

Bamboo sways with a silly twist,
Finding pleasure in the mist.
A frog hops up, a grand encore,
Croaking jokes I've never heard before.

Each glance reveals a playful scene,
Where laughter reigns, so fresh, so green.
In this odd zoo that feels so right,
I laugh with critters day and night.

Moss-Kissed Memories Through Glass

Raindrops tap a cheeky tune,
As ferns wave like they're immune.
A window world of frolicsome cheer,
Where nature smiles, no room for fear.

Silly shadows in the glow,
Dance around in gentle flow.
A sloth just winked, a friendly tease,
I giggled loud, oh what a breeze!

Squirrels scurry, tails held high,
Plotting stunts up in the sky.
Each droplet tells a funny tale,
As to the jungle I exhale.

With every giggle, I connect,
To life outside, what a project!
Memories hug, so soft, so bright,
In this glass frame, pure delight.

Retreat into Greenery

Lost in layers of leafy stacks,
A raccoon stops to share some snacks.
He grins with crumbs upon his cheek,
While I ponder the joy critique.

The sun plays tricks through every vine,
Each ray a joke, a silly sign.
A toucan's beak, a colorful shock,
Makes me giggle at the tick-tock.

A grasshopper hops, a jittery jest,
Inviting a leap, oh what a quest!
I join the fun, swing low, swing high,
In this green place, I skip and fly.

With grinning leaves, my spirit's free,
In nature's arms, a jubilee.
Every twist, a swell of glee,
In this retreat, just you and me.

The Poetry of Leaves and Light

Leaves whisper secrets, soft and sweet,
While sunbeams dance to a funky beat.
A chameleon grins, a wily sprite,
Changing colors, what a sight!

A butterfly flutters, taking a chance,
Inviting me to join the dance.
With giggles hidden in each flutter,
A melody sweet as peanut butter.

The air is thick with juicy laughs,
As vines sway in silly drafts.
A boisterous breeze, a playful tease,
Oh, how I wish to be a breeze!

With every flicker, each playful thought,
This forest giggle, can't be bought.
In verses sung by trees so bright,
I find my muse in leaf and light.

Serenity Beyond the Glass

Behind the pane, the monkeys swing,
Chasing birds that chirp and sing.
A parrot squawks a cheeky joke,
As I stare and dream, my coffee smoke.

The lizards lounge, they take their seat,
No work for them, just sun and heat.
I sip my brew, they bask in cheer,
While noises of laughter drift near.

A squirrel leaps with a daring flair,
"My acorn stash? You didn't share!"
I chuckle softly at their fuss,
In my cozy nook, there's just us.

As the sun dips low, shadows grow,
These antics steal the evening show.
Nature's circus, wild and free,
A spectacle awaiting me!

Dappled Light and Lush Shadows

Peering out, I spy a trend,
A raccoon wearing a hat, my friend!
He waves his paw, so suave and sly,
With fruit loops strung together to dry.

A sloth moves slow, so lackadaisical,
His movement's like a comical miracle.
He scratches his belly, takes a snooze,
In this wacky world, who needs the blues?

Along the path, a goat's in a chase,
Chasing a butterfly, what a race!
He stumbles, tumbles into a bush,
Creating a hilarious, leafy hush.

With laughter and giggles, the day rolls on,
Through dappled light, spring's sweet song.
As critters parade in playful spree,
Life's a laugh, to watch and to be!

A Tapestry of Green Dreams

Canvas of leaves, a paintbrush divine,
Here, colors mix, and the rhythms align.
A frog in a top hat croaks his tune,
While a snail in shades says, "See you soon!"

Underneath ferns, the ants march stout,
In tiny boots, they wander about.
With crumbs they carry, a feast they lay,
Holding a banquet on this fine day.

A chameleon acts a prank so sly,
Changing hues in a blink of an eye.
"Did you see that?!" the toad exclaims,
As he rolls on the ground, calling names.

A tapestry weaved from laughter and glee,
Nature's wonders for you and for me.
In every twist, a grin goes wide,
Let's paint our dreams with joy and pride!

The Wild Heart Outside

The curtain sways with a lively breeze,
Outside, the chaos brings me to my knees.
A goat on a bike, yes, that's the sight,
I couldn't help but laugh at this silly delight.

A parrot, wise with tales to share,
Squawks about love, but mostly the fair.
"You ate my sandwich!" it caws in jest,
While I munch crumbs and laugh at the rest.

The sunbeams play, a patchwork of glee,
Oranges, yellows, in a dance spree.
Monkeys juggling in rhythmic style,
Make my days brighter with each little smile.

With every moment, nature's a song,
A symphony where funny things belong.
Wrapped in joy, I'll never hide,
In this wild heart, forever ride!

Enclosed by Flora and Fauna

In the corner, vines do creep,
A parrot chatters, never sleeps.
The tigers play with borrowed shoes,
While squirrels debate the evening news.

A monkey swings from curtain rail,
Leaves a trail like any tale.
The cactus rolls its prickly eyes,
As snails argue who's the prize.

The fern gives shade to weary gnomes,
Who dream of far-off, leafy homes.
Beneath the ferns, the spiders sing,
A tune that makes the noonday swing.

With laughter echoing through the room,
The flowers sway in joyful bloom.
Together they dance, a leafy crew,
Creating fun in every hue.

Whispers of the Earth's Heartbeat

A turtle wrote a book of lore,
While crickets held a "dance-off" war.
The worms debated who was fast,
As daisies laughed and bloomed at last.

The frogs croaked jokes of ancient times,
While ants concocted silly rhymes.
The night was bright, the stars were queer,
As raccoons shared their stash of beer.

A racquet's lost, lost in the fray,
The plants now join the games we play.
With roots that tap and stems that sway,
The dance of nature does not delay.

The sunbeams sneak through leaves above,
Creating shadows, all in love.
And laughter fills the air with light,
In this silly world, all feels right.

Rhythms of the Unseen Wild

A beat from paws, a chirp from beak,
In this wild place, shenanigans peak.
The raccoons toss leaves high in the sky,
While tree frogs join them, oh me, oh my!

With fireflies painting twinkling trails,
As owls hoot out their funny tales.
The bunnies dance in little shoes,
While hedgehogs laugh with silly views.

The night is alive with echoes clear,
As creatures gather, bringing cheer.
Each rustle in the brush a song,
In this whimsical place, we all belong.

A pelican struts, quite the sight,
With a silly grin, oh what a delight.
Together they share in this amusing throng,
Where the heart of earth sings bold and strong.

Glass Barriers and Verdant Dreams

Behind the glass, the world's a play,
A lizard's wiggle, a bird's ballet.
The chattering geckos quiz the day,
While butterflies host a snazzy buffet.

The sun reflects on leafy screens,
As goofballs swim in dewy greens.
The mice have formed a secret club,
Complete with cheese and a garden hub.

A tarantula tells jokes so grand,
With spider silk, they make a band.
The petals chuckle, the weeds cartwheel,
In this playful realm, joy is real.

Where every blink reveals a scene,
Of quirky creatures, oh so keen.
And laughter rings inside that space,
In this vibrant, silly, leafy place.

Wild Heartbeats Beyond the Frame

A monkey flips and makes a show,
Right past the glass, he steals the show.
The parrot squawks, a vibrant hue,
While squirrels plan their grand debut.

A snake slides down, oh what a sight,
He's tangled up, in sheer delight.
The kids are laughing, oh what a tease,
As nature dances with playful ease.

A raccoon sneaks with mischief's flair,
While butterflies scatter everywhere.
Hilarity reigns in this wild scene,
As laughter echoes, bright and keen.

Enchantment of the Wilderness View

In the distance, a tiger yawns wide,
While a gopher bursts forth, full of pride.
The deer on the lawn do twist and twirl,
As the breeze sends daisies into a whirl.

A giraffe peeks in, with a neck so long,
He's taken a shine to our neighborhood throng.
The cat next door hides, a bit dismayed,
While the wild crowd plays, unafraid.

A lily pad floats like a raft in the air,
The frogs join in, without a care.
With grins all around, it feels just right,
As our window show lights up the night.

Fluttering Leaves and Daydreams

The leaves are dancing, oh what a sight,
Caught in the breezes, in pure delight.
A squirrel prances, with acorn in tow,
As if he's starring in a grand show.

The sun peeks through, making shadows play,
While the chipmunks scamper, never delay.
With every rustle, the wild tales unfold,
In the air, there's laughter, brightly bold.

The flowers giggle, colors that pop,
As ants march by, never a stop.
Nature's antics, behind the glass,
In this whimsical world, we raise a glass.

Nature's Symphony on the Sill

The crickets chirp a tune so sweet,
While the goldfish swims, tapping his feet.
The wind blows soft, a gentle hum,
In this symphony, we all join in.

Clouds drift by, in silly shapes,
A spaceship, a hat, maybe some grapes!
As the day fades, the fireflies spark,
They twirl and dance, igniting the dark.

A bear takes a bow, with a playful grin,
While the owls hoot, inviting us in.
Nature plays on, with laughter and cheer,
Each note a reminder, to hold it near.

Silhouettes of Wilderness

In the corner, a parrot snickers,
A monkey swings, untamed by stickers.
Chasing shadows on the wall,
They plan their escape, heedless of the call.

Lizards dance in a vibrant line,
While squirrels plot over acorn brine.
The jokes they tell are quite absurd,
As I sip tea, with little heard.

A lion's roar shatters my calm,
But it's just a cat, oh how charming and palm!
They giggle like humans with a silly shout,
In this wild gallery, there's never a doubt.

So here I sit, amazed and bold,
In this comedy where nature unfolds.
Each creature's laugh, a rhythm divine,
In the corner of my room where wild meets wine.

The Breath of Vines Within

Vines creep up, tickling my toes,
A snail has dreams, as time slows.
The air's a joke, thick with delight,
As frogs stage a concert in the moonlight.

I spy a sloth, grinning wide,
In a hammock made of leaves, it'll bide.
Swaying along to breezy tunes,
A comedic star beneath the moons.

Old trees chuckle, shaking their trunks,
As wisps of wind poke the funky punks.
A troupe of ants in a feathery march,
Govern their kingdom on a crumbzy arch.

Laughter echoes through the green maze,
Nature's humor is truly a blaze.
In this realm of vine and glee,
I find my muse, forever free.

Serenity in Leafy Light

A turtle slips with a goofy glide,
While grasshoppers hop with pride.
The sun beats down in a jolly play,
Spilling laughter in a leafy array.

Butterflies flutter, wearing their best,
As the wind whispers, 'You're a guest!'
The flowers giggle, pink and bright,
Joining the fun, basking in light.

Crickets sing in their fancy attire,
While shadows lengthen like a comic choir.
The grass giggles as the breeze combs,
Tickled by whispers of faraway homes.

In this bright fest, I lose my woe,
With every chuckle, I'm ready to go.
Leafy laughter fills my core,
In nature's arms, I can't ask for more.

Treetops in the Twilight

It's a monkey's circus up high in the trees,
Swinging and flipping with utmost ease.
The owls hoot jokes from their spindly perch,
While the humor flows like a comic search.

Stars peek out, giggling away,
As fireflies join in the dance and play.
A raccoon rumbles through messy bins,
Searching for treasures, with laughing grins.

The moon shimmers on a playful breeze,
Whispering secrets with ancient ease.
Tall trees tremble, trying to contain,
The chuckles of life, flowing like rain.

In twilight's glow, I cannot help but beam,
In this playful world, I dare to dream.
Nature's comedy, a delightful spin,
In the canopy where the fun begins.

www.ingramcontent.com/pod-product-compliance
Lightning Source LLC
Chambersburg PA
CBHW050305120526
44590CB00016B/2496